SPOTLIGHT ON S⊙CCER

SOCCER PLAYERS AND SKILLS

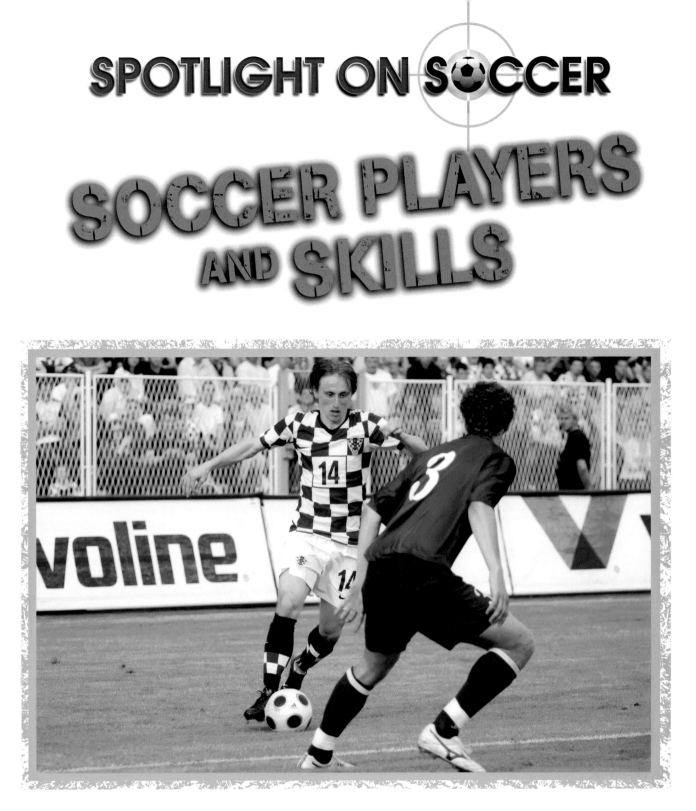

Clive Gifford

PowerKids press.

New York

Published in 2011 by The Rosen Publishing Group Inc.
29 East 21st Street, New York, NY 10010

First Edition

Editor: Julia Adams
Produced by: Tall Tree Ltd.
Editor, Tall Tree: Jon Richards
Designer: Ben Ruocco

Library of Congress Cataloging-in-Publication Data

Gifford, Clive.
    Soccer players and skills / by Clive Gifford. -- 1st ed.
        p. cm. -- (Spotlight on soccer)
    Includes index.
    ISBN 978-1-61532-611-2 (library binding)
    ISBN 978-1-61532-612-9 (paperback)
    ISBN 978-1-61532-616-7 (6-pack)
    1. Soccer--Training--Juvenile literature. I. Title.
    GV943.9.T7G55 2010
    796.334--dc22
                                            2009045774

Photographs
All photographs taken by Michael Wicks, except;
t—top, l—left, r—right, b—bottom, c—center
cover t—Dreamstime.com, tr—Dreamstime.com/
Moori, bl—Dreamstime.com/Putnik70, tl—Dreamstime.
com/Miflippo, c—Dreamstime.com/Ginosphotos,
1 Dreamstime.com/Lario Tus, 2 Dreamstime.com/
Fabrizio Mariani, 4 Dreamstime.com/Santamaradona,
5 Dreamstime.com/Diademimages, 6 Dreamstime.
com/Jose Gil, 7 Mitchell Layton/NewSport/Corbis, 8
Dreamstime.com/Diademimages, 15 Duomo/Corbis, 17
Dreamstime.com/Diademimages, 18 Dreamstime.com/
Diademimages, 20 Dreamstime.com/Fabrizio Mariani, 25
Dreamstime.com/Lario Tus, 28 Dreamstime.com/Dong Hj,
30 Dreamstime.com/Diademimages, 32 Dreamstime.com/
Diademimages

Acknowledgements
The author and publisher would like to thank the following people for their help and participation in this book: Whiteknights FC, Eric Burrow, Steve Rendell, and Paul Scholey.

Manufactured in China.
CPSIA Compliance Information: Batch #WAS0102PK: For Further Information contact
Rosen Publishing, New York, New York at 1-800-237-9932

CONTENTS

A Sport of Skill

Soccer is a sport full of excitement, energy, and drama where matches can be won and lost in a split-second. Soccer players need to develop the skills necessary to take part. These skills include the ability to control the ball, as well as how to spot gaps and weaknesses in the opposing team.

Field and Players

A soccer field measures up to 130 yards (120 m) long and 76 yards (70 m) wide. With 22 players on two sides competing for the ball, even this large area can still feel crowded. Players try to space themselves out by playing in various positions, such as defense, midfield, and attack. Players in different positions need different skills—defenders must be strong tacklers, attackers must be good at shooting.

A goalkeeper practices saving shots during training. Goalkeepers need different skills from other players on the field. They need to be agile in order to make diving saves and they need to be good at catching the ball.

Starting Out

Many soccer stars began playing for fun with their friends in the streets and parks and on the beaches near their homes. Small-team games, such as five-a-side, help to build basic skills. These skills are then worked on with coaches in training at schools and clubs. As players progress and play for better and better teams, they never stop practicing their core skills, even if they get to play for their countries. These skills include being able to pass quickly and accurately with both feet, control the ball as they twist and turn, shoot strongly, and head the ball well.

> *I think the best way to improve your skills is to play football [soccer] on a smaller pitch [field]. I didn't play 11-a-side football until I was 13. On a small pitch, you need to have good control and move the ball around quickly. There isn't much space so you need to be skillful.*
>
> Brazilian soccer star, **Juninho**

The French soccer player, Franck Ribéry (in blue), runs at two Dutch defenders during a 2006 international match. Ribéry has great skills and balance, and is known for running at opponents with the ball under close control.

Fit and Fast

Soccer is an athletic, high-intensity sport, so players need to be very fit to perform at their best throughout a match. Even the most expert players have to practice their skills and improve their fitness.

In Training

Professional soccer players undergo different types of training to develop their physical fitness, strength, and skills. Players work on their strength and stamina in the gym and in outdoor sessions. Pace is very important in soccer, which is why training will include sprinting practice. Players also perform drills and play small games while training, in order to develop skills such as shooting, tackling, and passing. These drills are performed under the watchful eye of the team's coach.

> " *Do you have the heart to push yourself? If you don't, find a way to get it, because talent will only get you so far.* "
>
> United States striker, **Tiffeny Milbrett**

Chelsea (UK) players warm up before a training session by lightly jogging around the field. Warming up is a vital part of training because it prepares a player's muscles, lungs, and heart for the hard exercise ahead.

Injuries and Prevention

Soccer injuries are a concern for players and teams—an injured player will not be able to play, possibly for a long time. Most injuries happen to the ankle and knee joints or the leg muscles. They can vary from a dead leg (a leg feeling numb because of a collision) to broken bones or torn ligaments. Such serious injuries can see a player unable to play for many months. Warming up and performing a lot of stretches before a match or heavy training session can prevent a lot of muscle injuries.

American player Brandi Chastain had to walk with crutches after breaking a bone in her right foot during a Women's World Cup match.

Playing Positions

A soccer team is divided into the goalkeeper and the 10 outfield players, who line up in a pattern called a formation. This pattern consists of rows of defenders, midfielders, and attackers.

Defenders

Defenders are expected to stop opposition attacks, so they need to be good at heading, marking (see page 20), and clearances (kicking or heading the ball away from their own goal). They should also be very skilled at anticipating an opponent's movement and making committed, decisive challenges without fouling the attacking opposition player.

ON THE BALL

Defenders can help their forward by joining an attack. Dutch defender Ronald Koeman scored a staggering 207 goals during his career, including 14 for his national team.

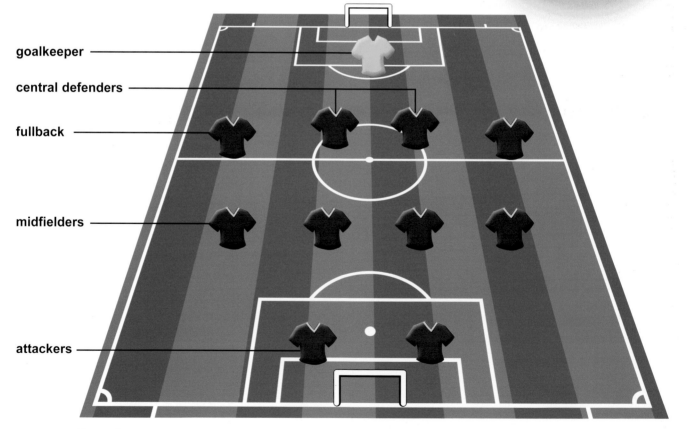

- goalkeeper
- central defenders
- fullback
- midfielders
- attackers

Team formations are described by the numbers of defenders, midfielders, and attackers, so the formation shown here is known as 4-4-2 (four defenders, four midfielders, and two attackers).

Midfielders and Attackers

Midfielders need to work on their fitness, since they help out both in defense and attack, covering more ground than any other players. They will receive a lot of passes as the ball moves back and forth between defense and attack, so they should be good at controlling the ball. Attackers need to be very good at scoring goals. They should be able to shoot and head the ball accurately, and they should also be able to spot good positions on the field where they will be in space to receive a pass and launch an attack.

Manchester United and England attacker Wayne Rooney (in white) gets past the tackle of a United States defender. Rooney has developed the skills needed to be a good attacker, so he is able to shoot from long distances and get into spaces from where he can score.

Passing

Quick passing can see a team keep the ball, move it past opponents, and get into a position to score. Passing is the most common skill used in a game. During one Euro 2008 match, Holland and Romania together made a staggering 1,040 passes—that is one pass every five seconds.

> "Football [soccer] is a simple game based on the giving and taking of passes, of controlling the ball, and of making yourself available to receive a pass.
>
> Legendary Liverpool soccer manager, **Bill Shankly**"

Longer Passing and Weight

Sometimes during a match you might want to send a pass across the entire width of the field. The high, lofted pass is best for this, using the top of the foot (where the shoelaces are) to lift the ball off the ground and send it over a long distance. You should get your body over the ball and swing your leg through the ball so that your shoelaces strike the middle of it. The amount of force put into a pass is called its weight. Getting the weight of a pass right is very important, especially when passing the ball ahead of another player for them to run onto. Too much weight can see the ball go out of play. Too little, and an opposing player could intercept the pass.

Lofted Pass

To make a lofted pass, this player has hit the ball with the top of her shoe. She has also leaned back, which will put more height onto her pass.

Sidefoot Pass

1 These two players are taking part in a simple drill to practice their sidefoot passes. Player 1 is passing to player 2. He turns his kicking foot sideways and makes contact with the ball using the side of his foot.

2 After player 1 has made contact with the ball, he follows through, pushing his foot, which is still turned sideways, toward player 2 to make sure that the pass is accurate. Player 2 will make a sidefoot pass back.

Short Passes

The most common pass in soccer is the sidefoot pass. This sees the ball rolled across the field using the inside of the shoe. Because the whole side of the foot comes into contact with the ball, it is the most accurate pass, but is best used over shorter distances. Flick passes can change the ball's direction. Flicks are usually made with the outside of the shoe. They have very little power and are used only over short distances.

Player Power

It is vital that you work hard at passing with both feet. During a match, you may not have the time or space to use your favored foot. Being able to pass with both feet allows you to move the ball all over the field and makes it harder for opponents to challenge you.

Flick Pass

To make a flick pass, this player is using the outside of his shoe. The kicking foot is swiveled quickly at the ankle. This nudges, or flicks, the ball to one side.

Ball Control

The receiver is the player to whom a pass is made. In some situations, a receiver's first touch of the ball is an immediate pass or header to a teammate. Usually, though, the receiving player first aims to control the ball in order to make a pass, shoot, or run.

Cushioning

You can use any part of your body to control the ball, with the exception of your hands and arms. If you do use your hands or arms, the referee will signal handball and the opposition will be awarded a free kick. However, if you handle the ball in your own penalty area and your action was considered deliberate, the opposition will be awarded a penalty and you could receive a yellow card or even a red card. To control the ball and slow it down, players use a skill called cushioning. The part of the body making contact with the ball is moved away from the ball as it arrives. This will slow the ball's impact and leave it under control at your feet. Cushioning using the side of the foot, the top of the thigh, and the chest are the most common.

This player is receiving a pass and bringing it under control using his foot. As the ball arrives, he moves his right foot back down with the ball to slow the ball's fall, so that it drops at his feet and under control.

Thigh Control

This player is controlling a pass using his thigh. The player raises his thigh to meet the ball and then pulls it down with the ball to slow the ball's fall.

Chest Control

1 If the pass is quite high, you might have to use your chest to control the ball. As the pass arrives, this player sticks out his chest to receive the ball.

2 Just as the ball arrives, the player pulls back his chest to cushion the ball. At the same time, he brings his shoulders forward to stop the ball bouncing off to one side.

Firm Control

In some situations, players try not to stop the ball dead, but change its direction instead. This is known as firm control. The part of the body that connects with the ball is kept firm and thrust forward as the ball arrives. By using firm control, a player can, for example, make a rapid pass over a short distance with their chest, twisting the upper body to steer the ball in the right direction.

Shielding, Running, and Turning

Once a player has received and controlled the ball, they need to make their next move. In many situations, the player may shield the ball, run, or turn with the ball.

Shielding

Sometimes, a player will receive a pass and immediately find themselves under pressure from an opponent. They can either pass the ball before the opponent can challenge them or protect the ball by shielding it. This is where the player puts their body between the opponent and the ball while keeping the ball under control. Keeping control of the ball is vital. If the player is not close to the ball and they use their body in this way, the referee will signal obstruction and award a free kick to the opposition.

ON THE BALL

Top players can run more than 6 miles (10 km) during a 90-minute match. At Euro 2008, Dutch midfielder Rafael van der Vaart ran 9.15 miles (14.73 km) during a single game.

Shielding the Ball

1 This attacker (in blue) is in possession of the ball and the defender (in yellow) stands close by to try to slow him down.

2 The attacker makes sure that he keeps himself between the defender and the ball, shielding it with his body.

3 While shielding the ball, the attacker can make a short pass to a teammate on one side or the other.

Running and Turning

A player running with the ball tries to keep their body in between the ball and any arriving opponent. When free of opposition players, they may push the ball in front, ready to change direction or to protect the ball. If they have a lot of space in front of them and no opponents within close range, a player may push the ball farther ahead so that they can sprint harder. They try to keep their head up, watching where teammates and opponents are in order to work out their next move. There are several ways that a player with the ball can turn to change direction. They can pivot around with one foot on the ball, or they can overrun the ball, cut back, and change direction quickly.

Abby Wambach of Washington Freedom shows good technique while running with the ball. Her head is up and she is looking around for any of her teammates to pass to and for any opposition players who may try to challenge her.

Crossing and Heading

A cross is a long, high pass from near the sidelines into the penalty area. Crosses are very useful for getting the ball behind the defenders and close to goal, where attackers are more likely to score.

Crossing Options

Crosses are aimed a little above head height, so that a teammate can run in and head the ball. The player crossing the ball needs to be aware of teammates' positions before making a cross. Sometimes, it may not be possible to cross the ball right away. There may be a defender blocking the ball's path or no teammates in the penalty area to aim for. In these situations, a player may try to sprint past a defender down the sideline before making a cross.

Crossing into the Penalty Area

1 Here, a player is making a cross from near the side of the field, using his left foot to make a lofted pass (see page 10). By leaning back, he gets plenty of height onto his cross.

2 The high ball puts taller attackers at an advantage. The tall attacker (in blue) can easily jump higher than shorter defenders and head the ball toward the goal.

Heading the Ball

During a match, the ball will spend a lot of time in the air, so heading is a vital skill in attack and defense. Players aim to meet the middle of the ball with their forehead and try to watch the ball right up to the moment of impact. A defensive header is aimed high and with as much power as possible to clear the ball. An attacking header toward goal sees the player try to get their head above the ball so that they can direct it down and away from the goalkeeper.

" *The art of heading for goal is to use your whole body to get as much power into your header as you can. Don't just let the ball bounce off your head. Use your whole body by bending your knees, arching your back, and tensing your neck muscles, and then thrust forward on contact.* "

Manchester United midfielder, **Gary Neville**

Even players who are experts at controlling the ball with their feet must learn to head the ball with confidence and power. Portugal and Manchester United winger Cristiano Ronaldo (in red) is well known for his dribbling skills, but he is also a superb header of the ball.

Goalkeeping

Goalkeepers need a lot of concentration, bravery, and lightning reactions. Top keepers alert their teammates to danger. They also take control when defending corners and free kicks, telling defenders where to go.

Positioning and Handling

While spectacular diving saves are the most memorable part of goalkeepers' play, most of their work involves being in the right position when the opposition attacks and making sure that they catch any crosses cleanly. Keepers aim to get their bodies in line with the direction of the ball. This means that their bodies form a second barrier if the ball bounces out of their hands. Once the ball is in their hands, goalkeepers can roll the ball out underarm, throw it out overarm, or kick it from their hands.

Miguel Calero of the Mexican team Pachuca makes a dramatic save against U.S. team DC United. Goalkeepers must be supple and athletic to pull off such difficult saves.

Catches, Punches, Deflections

Keepers practice catching the ball at different heights and angles. These catches range from stretching up to grab a high ball to dropping on one knee to gather in a ball rolling across the field. At all times during a game, a keeper focuses on the play, watching the ball and always prepared for an attack. Sometimes, a keeper decides they cannot catch the ball securely. In these cases, they make a punch to clear the ball or deflect it over the crossbar or around the post.

That's what goalkeeping is all about. It's really having nothing to do at times, and then having to make sure you are concentrating and ready to make the save when called upon.

United Statess goalkeeper,
Kasey Keller

Goalkeeping Practice

Catching high balls (above) requires plenty of concentration. The keeper should watch the ball all the way into his hands, to stop it from slipping out.

When fielding a low ball (above), the keeper drops to one knee and gets his body behind the ball to create a second barrier behind his hands. He watches the ball right into his hands.

Kicking is an important part of keeping (left), since a keeper may have to clear the ball quickly when challenged by the opposition.

Tackling and Defending

Players have to defend when they lose possession of the ball. They must cut down the space their opponents have to attack, stop goals from being scored, and try to recover the ball.

Marking and Blocking

Defenders stick close to individual opponents and follow their movements to prevent them getting into space to receive a pass. This is called marking. When an opponent does have the ball, the aim is to stop them turning to face goal. Defenders may sometimes jump in the way to block a shot or an attacking pass.

Defenders have to work together as a unit to stop attacks. Here, the defenders of Siena (in black and white) are closing down Clarence Seedorf from AC Milan (in red) during an Italian Serie A game.

Tackling

When a player challenges for the ball, they need to be strong and decisive. The front block is the most common form of tackle (see right). Another is the side tackle (see below). When an opponent is running with the ball, it may be possible to kick the ball out of their control using a side tackle. Defenders try to stay on their feet. The sliding tackle sees defenders slide along the ground, and it is used only as a last resort. With all tackles, care has to be taken to connect with the ball and not the attacking player, otherwise the defender will be given a foul and the opposition will be awarded a free kick.

Front Block

1 The defender (in yellow) places his left foot firmly, bending the knee slightly to get his weight over the ball.

2 He then strikes the ball with his right foot, knocking it away, while making sure not to touch the attacker.

Side Tackle

1 The defender (in yellow) picks his moment to tackle carefully so as not to get a foul.

2 He moves in and makes a firm challenge for the ball using the side of his foot.

3 Taking care not to foul the attacker, he knocks the ball clear.

The defender (in yellow) has chosen to use a sliding tackle. Sliding tackles are very risky and take a lot of skill, so they should be performed only as a last resort. The defender slides in on his left leg, extending his right leg to clear the ball out of the control of his opponent.

21

Attacking Skills

Attackers with the ball have a lot of responsibility. They do not want to give the ball away easily, but they also want to continue the attack, taking the ball into more dangerous positions to try to score.

Attacking Techniques

While passing can create chances to score, there are other techniques that attackers can use as well. A player can fake a pass to trick a defender into moving the wrong way, before driving forward with the ball and taking a shot. Another way of beating an opponent is called the push-and-go. This works only if there is a lot of space behind an opponent. The attacker pushes the ball past the defender and into the open space. They then sprint hard to collect the ball. A variation of this move, known as a nutmeg, involves passing the ball between the defender's legs.

Balance and control are very important when attacking with the ball. Here, players are practicing their dribbling skills by moving the ball in and out through a line of poles.

Dribbling and Tricks

Dribbling is moving while keeping the ball under close control with a series of nudges and taps. It is very risky and should be performed only in areas close to the other team's goal. Players such as Cristiano Ronaldo and Arjen Robben are highly skilled at adding swerves, stepovers, and changes of speed and direction to their dribbling. The aim is to confuse or unbalance a defender, making it easier to dribble and sprint past them.

> *It is important when dribbling to use both feet. Make sure you use the outside, inside, and soles of your feet. Make sure you stay on your toes, bend your knees, and keep your head up.*
>
> England winger,
> **Rachel Yankey**

Stepovers

1 As the ball is rolling forward, the attacker moves his left foot over the ball, taking care not to touch it.

2 When the left foot comes down, the attacker's right foot moves around behind the ball.

3 The attacker places his left foot and can now change direction, moving the ball away quickly to his right.

4 Alternatively, he can step over the ball again, this time with his right foot, to try to confuse and unbalance a nearby defender and make him lunge for the ball.

Movement and Vision

Attacking players should always try to make attacking runs, from where they can create opportunities to score. They should also get into positions away from defenders where they can receive a pass and launch an attack.

Getting Free

Any attacking run must be well timed and performed sharply to shake off a defender standing close by. Attackers use changes of direction and vary their running speed to get free of a defender. Another technique is to fake intentions. This is when an attacker leans one way and appears to be heading in that direction, but sprints away in a different direction instead.

ON THE BALL

In 2008, David Beckham, playing for the United States team, LA Galaxy, showed great technique and awareness to score with a shot 66 yards (60 m) from the goal.

Chipping Over the Defense

1 The attackers (in blue) are aiming to get behind the defender (in yellow). Attacker 1 chooses to play a short lofted kick, called a chip, over the top of the defender.

2 Attacker 1 stabs down with his foot on the bottom half of the ball to chip it over the defender's head. Attacker 2 times his run to meet the pass. The ball and the attacker are now behind the defender and the attack can be continued.

Width and Vision

Using the sides, or flanks, of the field is a great way to get the ball behind a defense. Attackers can make overlapping runs down the flanks with the ball passed ahead of them to run onto. Players can work together to pass and move rapidly, using sharp running and quick, precise touches to move the ball around the field and past defenders. In order to perform these moves successfully, however, players must have vision. This is an awareness of what is going on around them and the ability to spot a possible attacking pass or space to move into.

> **It's sometimes appropriate to pass to a teammate and I'll always do that. I guess a good striker will take the shot 80 percent of the time. But forwards have to know the best position and get there in the most efficient way. It's football [soccer] intelligence.**
>
> French attacker,
> **Fredi Kanouté**

Luka Modric of Croatia (in red and white) makes an attacking run against a Moldovan defender. Modric is well known for making such attacking runs and for his control of the ball with both feet. He is also very good at getting into attacking positions when he does not have the ball.

Shooting and Scoring

It is vital that all soccer players practice shooting and scoring goals accurately. All players, including defenders and midfielders, may get a chance to shoot during a match.

Player Power

All players, including world-class strikers, miss easy chances to score. Put a bad miss out of your mind and focus on taking the next chance you get to score.

Shooting Skills

Shooting relies on quick reactions to get a shot off before a defender can tackle or block. It also relies on good placement of the shot, such as aiming the ball away from the goalkeeper and toward the empty corners of the goal. Shooting too high is a common problem. This can often be corrected by getting the body over the ball and remembering not to lean back as the shot is made.

The easiest way to place a shot is using the side of the foot. However, this will not put a lot of power into the shot, so it should be used only at close range, as shown by this attacker (in blue).

Volleys and Other Shots

A ball struck while in midair is known as a volley. A well-struck volley can result in an unstoppable shot. A half-volley is where the ball is struck just as it bounces, but the resulting shot can be just as powerful as a volley. Shots are not always powerful drives and volleys. Chip shots are when players dig their kicking feet sharply into the bottom of the ball to send it up and over a goalkeeper. Other goals are scored when attackers, with their back to goal, simply backheel the ball into the net.

Hitting a Front-on Volley

1 As the ball arrives, the attacker keeps his eye on it and pulls back his shooting leg.

2 He keeps his kicking foot pointing down and he keeps his head over the ball to stop his shot from flying into the air.

3 He aims to strike the ball with his shoelaces, and after kicking the ball, his leg follows through.

Here, an attacker (in blue) has realized that he cannot reach a cross with his foot. As a result, he has thrown himself to perform a diving header and put the ball past the keeper.

Set-Piece Skills

Set pieces are ways of restarting a match after a stoppage or because the ball has gone off the field. Teams spend lots of time practicing set pieces, because they often result in a goal.

Free Kicks

A free kick is awarded to a team when opposition players have broken one of the game's rules. The team awarded the free kick can either shoot or pass the ball, depending on where the free kick has been awarded. Many free kicks see the ball launched high into the other team's penalty area. If the free kick is close to goal, the attacking players may try to shoot directly at the goal, bending or swerving the ball so that it curves around the edge of a defensive wall and toward goal.

A Chinese attacker (in red) has taken a free kick against Vietnam (in white). He has bent the ball over and around the wall of defenders shielding the goal.

Corners

A corner is awarded when the ball goes out of play across the goal line and a defender was the last player to touch the ball. Corners can be hit short to a nearby teammate or crossed long into the penalty area. A corner taker normally uses the lofted pass (see page 10) and tries to get enough height on the ball for a teammate to make a header. Teammates aim to time their runs so that they can meet the ball with a header at the goal.

> *Take a good look at your players and decide who can deliver the right ball. Decide what type of delivery you want, i.e., inswinger, outswinger, or just chipped to the near post, and choose who can deliver the ball.*
>
> West Ham United academy coach,
> **Tony Carr,** on taking corners

Taking Corners

1 As the player taking the corner moves in to cross the ball into the penalty area, his teammates try to get free of the defenders who are marking them.

2 The corner taker has the option to curve the ball in toward the goal (an inswinging corner) or away from the goal (an outswinging corner).

What It Takes To Be...

A Top Player

Marta Vieira da Silva

Marta was discovered while playing soccer at the age of 14. She gained experience and improved her skills in youth and the first teams of three Brazilian women's clubs. At 5 feet 1/2 inch (1.54 m) tall, Marta had to work hard to succeed against bigger, stronger opponents. She has played in midfield but is now renowned as a goal-scoring striker with pace, great dribbling, and a powerful shot.

Career Path

- ⚽ 2001 Wins the Under 19 Brazil Championship with Vasco da Gama team.

- ⚽ 2004 Moves to leading Swedish women's team, Umeå IK.

- ⚽ 2006 Voted by FIFA as the world's best female player at the age of 20.

- ⚽ 2008 Wins her third World Footballer of the Year title.

- ⚽ 2009 Moves to United States club Los Angeles Sol to play in the first season of Women's Professional Soccer.

During the 2007 Women's World Cup, Marta finished as the competition's top scorer and was voted its best player.

Glossary

chip lifting the ball over an opposition player by stabbing downward on the underside of the ball. Chips are used for short passes or for shots on goal.

coach someone who works with the players, deciding who should play and what tactics to use. A coach does not get involved in any business aspects of the soccer club.

corner awarded to an attacking team when the ball crosses the goal line and a defender was the last player to touch the ball. A corner is taken from inside a small quadrant in the corner of the field on the side where the ball went out of play.

dribbling running with the ball under control, nudging it forward using light touches so that it does not get too far ahead and out of control.

free kick a way of restarting a game. Referees award free kicks to a team when the opposition commits a foul or breaks one of the laws of the game.

marking to stand close to opposition players and follow their movements closely, making sure that they do not get into enough space to receive a pass.

nutmeg kicking the ball between the legs of an opposition player and collecting the ball on the other side.

set pieces ways of restarting a game after the ball has left play or a foul has been committed. Set pieces include free kicks, corners, and throw-ins.

striker a team's best goal scorer and the player who usually plays nearest the opposition goal.

Further Reading

Soccer Skills For Young Players
by Ted Buxton (Firefly Books, 2007)

Talking About Soccer: Goalkeeper
by Clive Gifford
(Sea to Sea Publications, 2007)

Talking About Soccer: Striker
by Clive Gifford
(Sea to Sea Publications, 2007)

Web Sites

Due to the changing nature of Internet links, PowerKids Press has developed an online list of Web sites related to the subject of this book. This site is updated regularly. Please use this link to access this list: http://www.powerkidslinks.com/sos/players

Index